DEAR dad

★ ★ ★ ★ ★ ★

KNOCK KNOCK®
VENICE, CALIFORNIA

Original text by Gerard Janssen
(and some of your own!)

Artwork by Petra Baan
(and some of your own!)

Originally published in Dutch by Uitgeverij Snor

Published in English by
Who's There Inc. d/b/a Knock Knock
Venice, CA 90291
knockknockstuff.com

Thanks to you I try my best at school. I hope to learn a lot and one day be able to write beautiful legalese too.

Made in China

The rights to this book have been negotiated by
the literary agency Sea of Stories
www.seaofstories.com

ISBN: 978-160106602-2
UPC: 825703-31051-1

10 9 8 7 6 5 4 3 2

This is kind of like a friendship book made by you for your dad. Of course, you and your dad aren't exactly real friends. But in some ways you still kind of are friends. Yay.

From your genius son/daughter:

____

____

(Write your name here.)

dear dad,

I'm so happy that you have so much fun stuff. This is what I like to play with the most:

Circle items you like to play with.

Oh, and also:

(Draw or paste items.)

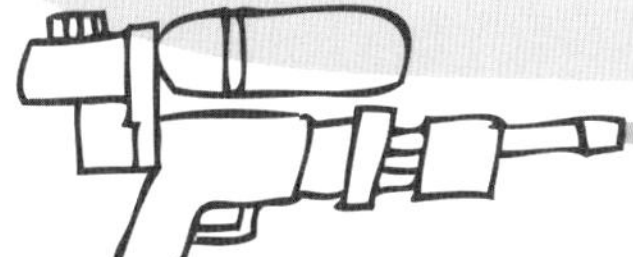

dear dad, *You look just like a:*

☐ *Lion tamer*

☐ *Astronaut*

☐ *Man with glasses*

☐ *Spy*

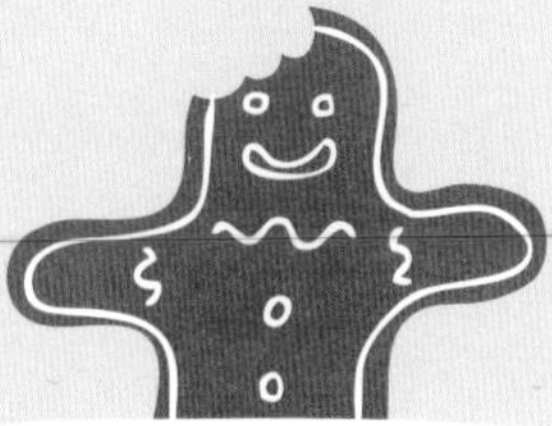

☐ *Gingerbread man*

☐ *Scientist with messy hair*

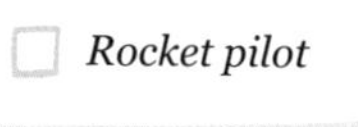

☐ *DJ*

☐ *Rocket pilot*

☐ *Singer*

My dad looks completely different than that! He looks like this:

Draw your dad here.

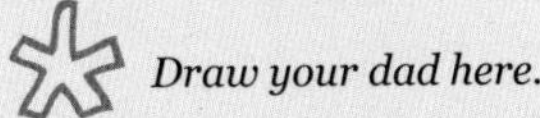

my father's name is:
But a better name for him would be:
Supersonic
Lionheart
Goblin
Tarzan
Gum-chewing Caveman

The Crane
Zeus
Mr. Cash
Beard Man
Sir Mustache
Oh, and also:

When the weather outside is awful,
this is what we do together:

- ☐ *Watch a movie*
- ☐ *Read comics*
- ☐ *Draw*
- ☐ *Color*
- ☐ *Horse around*
- ☐ *Bake a cake*
- ☐ *Build a pillow-and-blanket fort*
- ☐ *Play on your phone*

And other stuff, like:

(Write down things you like to do with your dad.)

My dad's mood goes like this, during the day:

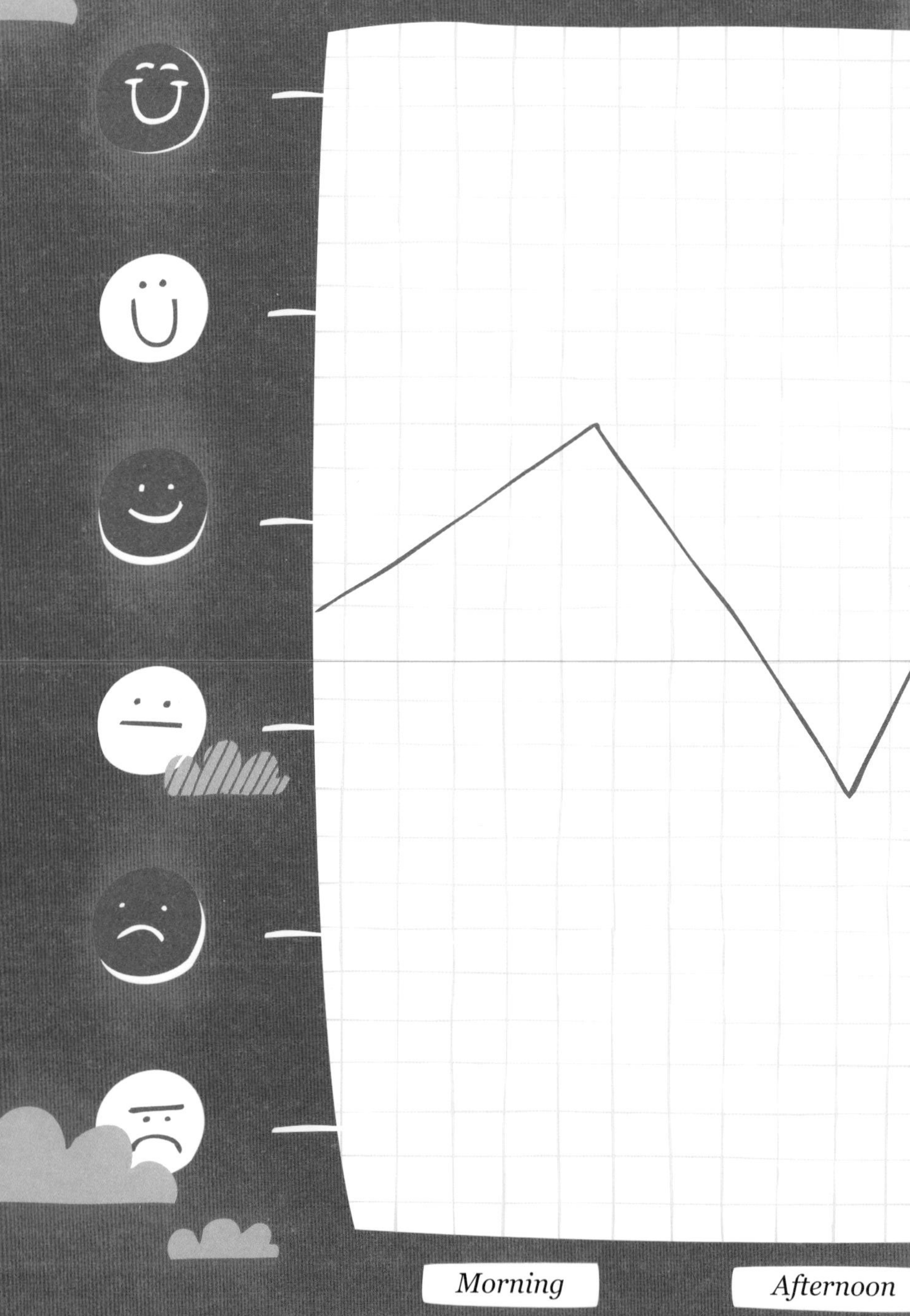

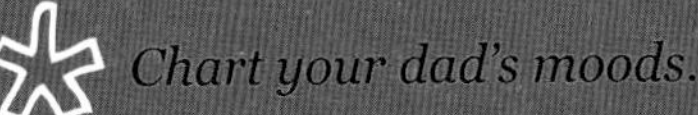

Chart your dad's moods.

Example

Dinnertime | *Bedtime* | *Sports-on-TV time*

When you're at work, this is what I think you do:

- ☐ *Read messages*
- ☐ *Write messages*
- ☐ *Work on the computer*
- ☐ *Play games*
- ☐ *Fire people*
- ☐ *Staple stuff*
- ☐ *Glue stuff*
- ☐ *Do math*
- ☐ *Read the newspaper*

Oh, and also:

(Write down what else you think your dad is busy doing at work.)

Here's all the stuff I think you can lift:

- ☐ *Me*
- ☐ *Mom*
- ☐ *Me and Mom*
- ☐ *A small UFO*
- ☐ *A Styrofoam house*
- ☐ *A fridge*
- ☐ *A cannonball*
- ☐ *A Japanese car*
- ☐ *A rubber boat*

Oh, and also:

Draw what else you think your dad can lift here!

When you tuck me in at night I feel like a...

Color in the item(s) you feel like when Dad tucks you in.

Oh, and also:

(Write how it feels when your dad tucks you in. Or just make a drawing!)

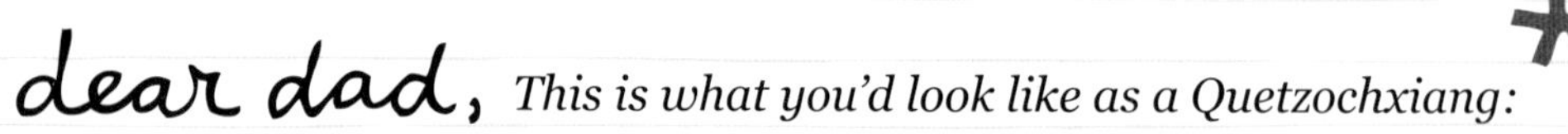
dear dad, This is what you'd look like as a Quetzochxiang:

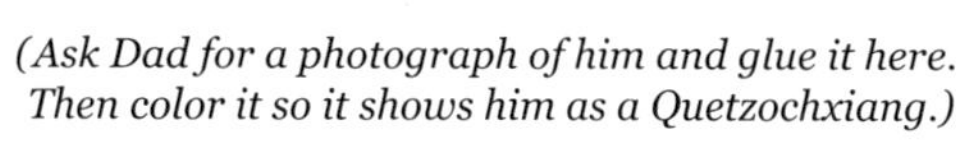
(Ask Dad for a photograph of him and glue it here.
Then color it so it shows him as a Quetzochxiang.)

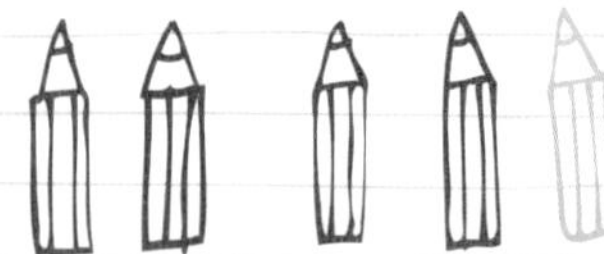

This is what I'd look like as a Quetzochxiang:

(Ask Dad for a photograph of you and glue it here. Then color it so it shows you as a Quetzochxiang.)

A Quetzochxiang is a creature from a faraway planet. It has eight legs, antlers, a very long pointy nose, two large teeth, and stripes.

dear dad, *I love seeing you dressed in:*

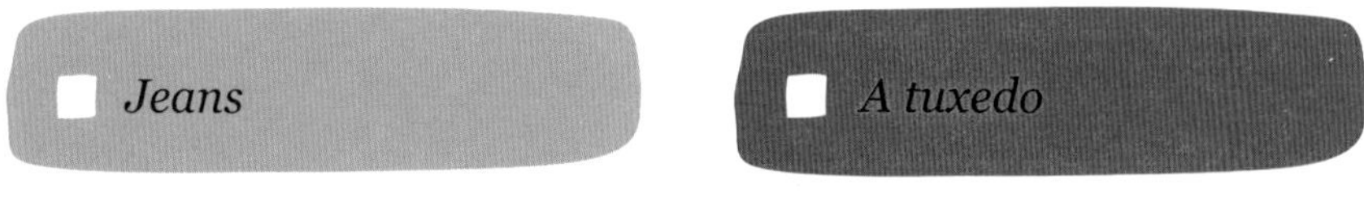

☐ *Halloween costume*

☐ *Pajamas*

☐ *Sports gear*

☐ *Suit of armor*

☐ *Uniform*

☐ *Bear suit*

Draw two cool new outfits for your dad here:

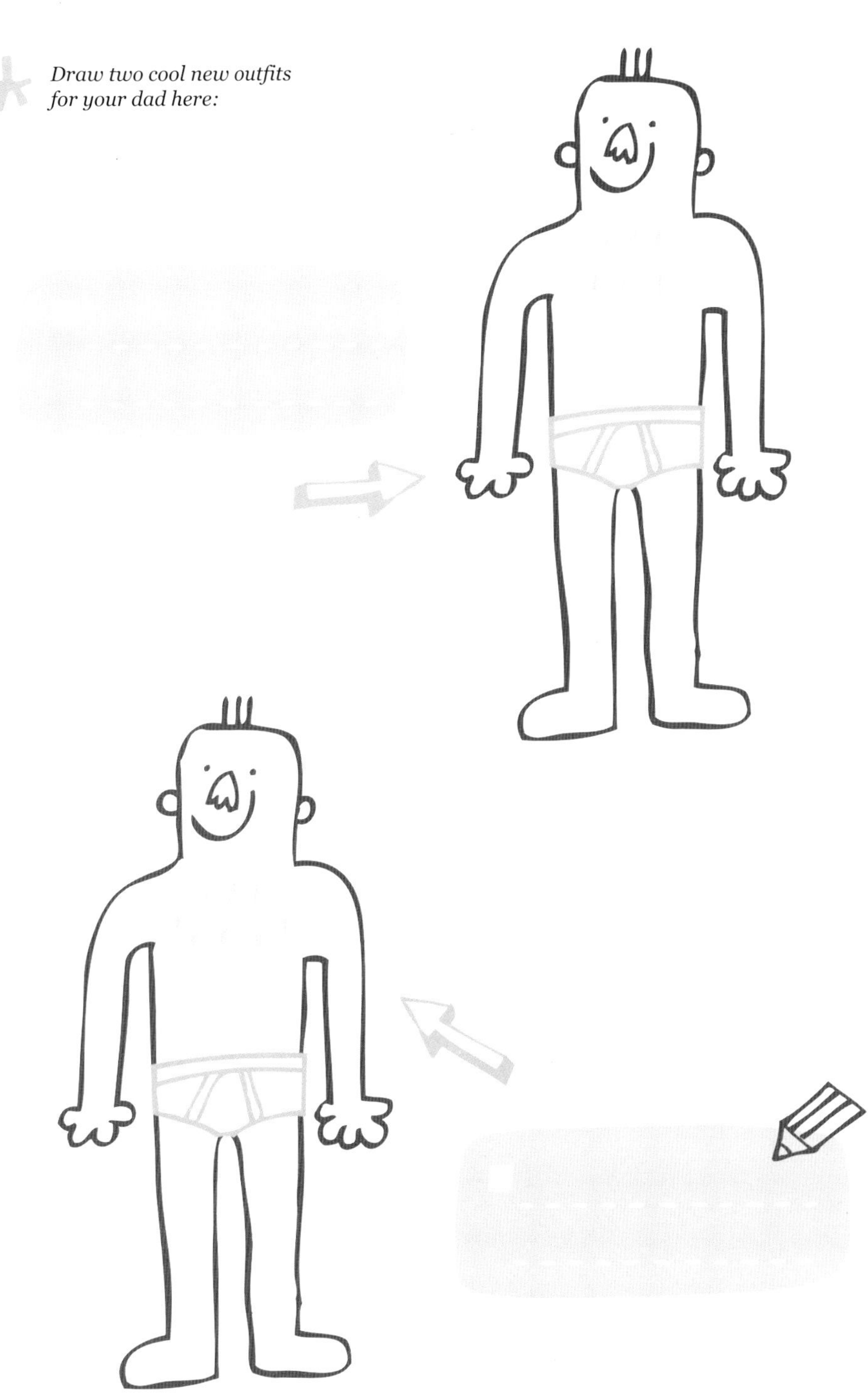

dear dad,

The most exciting thing that happened to us in the last year is:

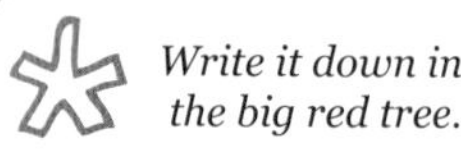

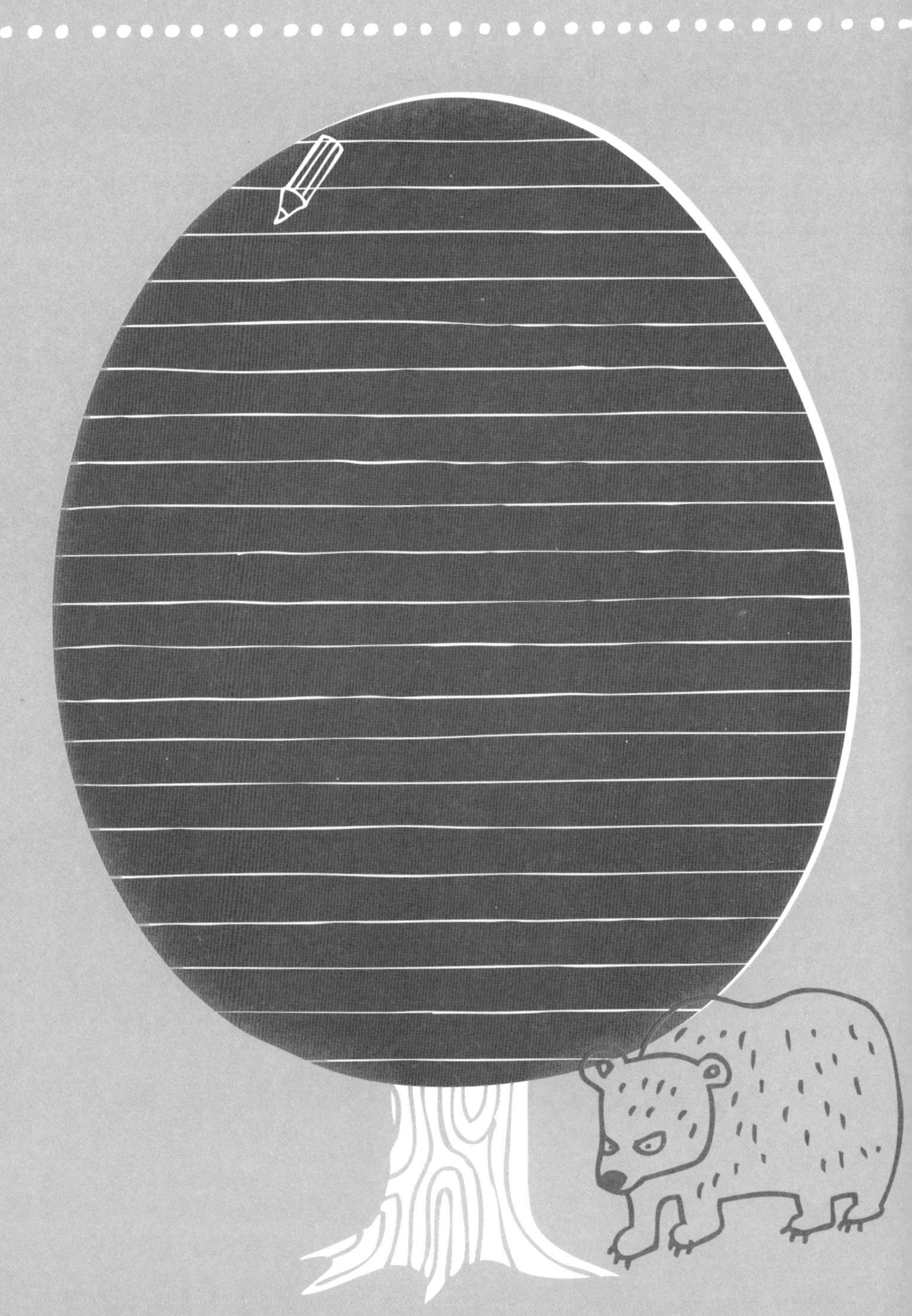

DEAR DAD,

You talk a lot about:

Color the item(s) your dad talks about most.

Oh, and also:

(Write or draw what your dad talks about most.)

I think this is your best joke:

You think this is my best joke:

dear dad, *I love it when you . . .*

- ☐ *imitate your boss*
- ☐ *shave*
- ☐ *pretend you're a monster*
- ☐ *dress up funny*
- ☐ *laugh*
- ☐ *say "oh, poop!"*

Oh, and also:

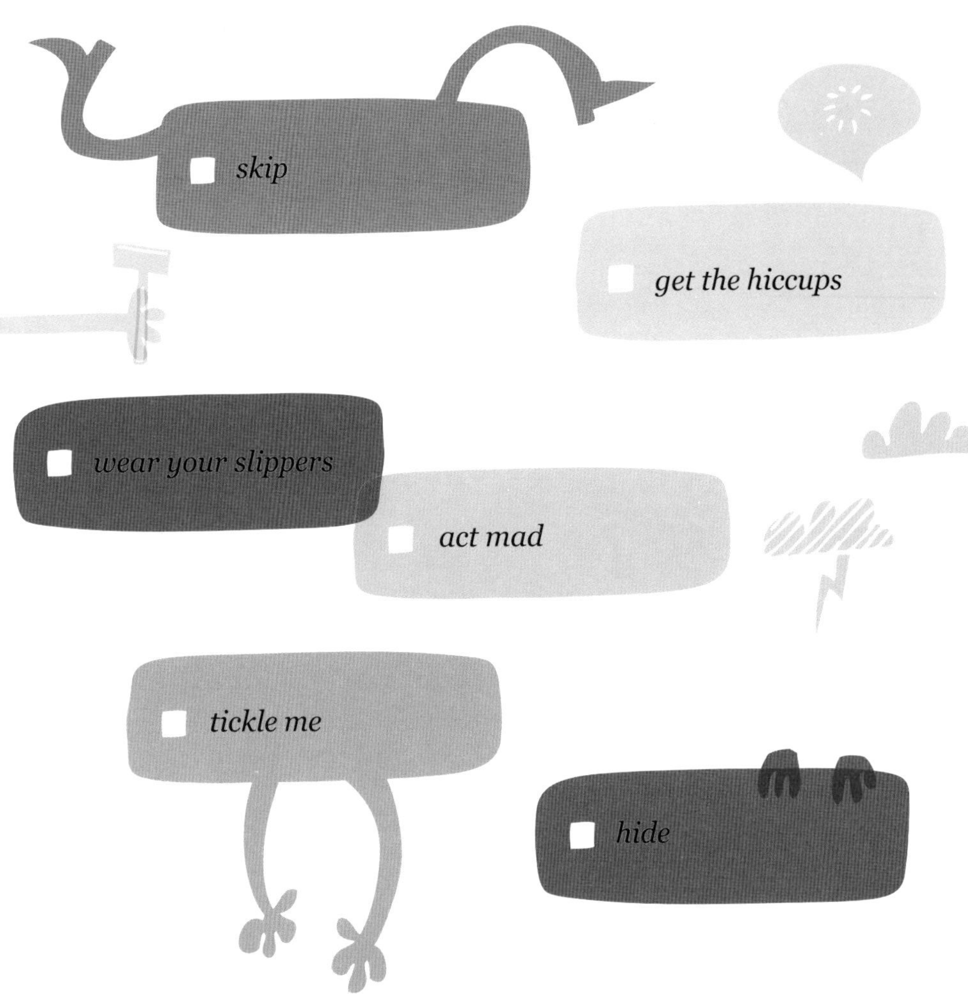

(Write other things your dad does that you like.)

The most fun day we've had together (so far!) was:

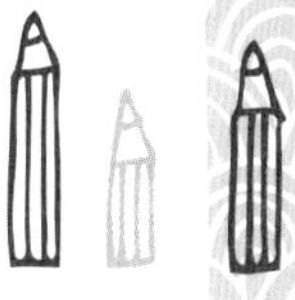

Draw pics of the stuff you and your dad did together that super-fun day.

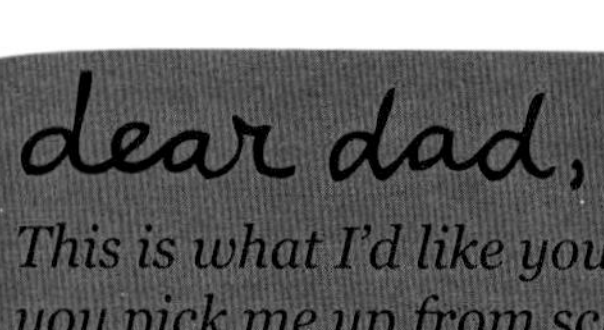

This is what I'd like you to wear when you pick me up from school:

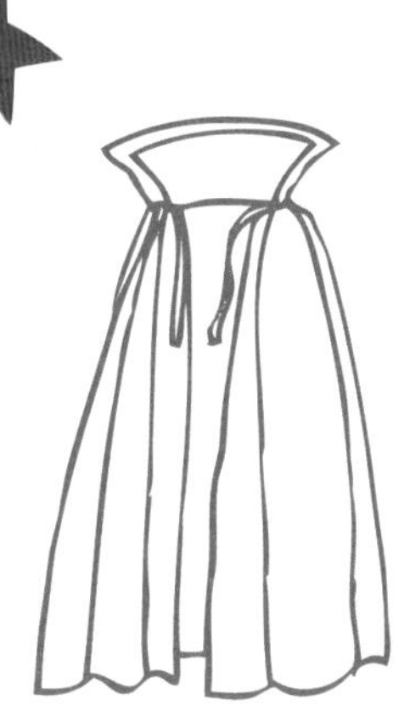

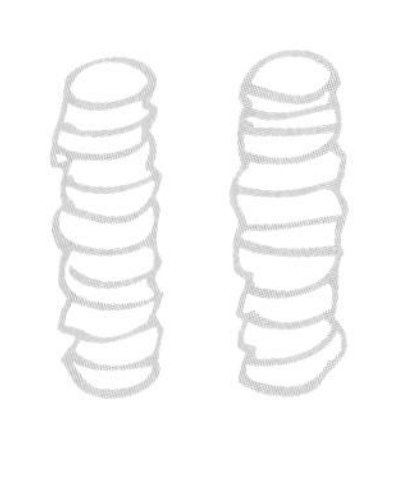

Color the clothes you'd like to see Dad in.

(Now, draw what you DON'T want your dad to wear!)

dear dad,

When I grow up, I want to be just as good as you at:

- ☐ *Driving a car*
- ☐ *Watching sports*
- ☐ *Playing with Legos*
- ☐ *Playing games*
- ☐ *Finding things*
- ☐ *Giving piggyback rides*
- ☐ *Flexing my abs*
- ☐ *Playing hopscotch*
- ☐ *Putting on a tie*
- ☐ *Grumbling*
- ☐ *Bird-watching*
- ☐ *Grilling on the BBQ*
- ☐ *Ironing*
- ☐ *Cheering on the sidelines*
- ☐ *Catching fish*
- ☐ *Swimming underwater*

Oh, and also:

(Draw or paste pics of what you want to be really good at someday.)

When I'm grown up like you I'd like to have:

- [ ] *An adult-sized nose*

- [ ] *Adult-sized ears*

- [ ] *Dad glasses*

- [ ] *A mustache*

Check off and draw the things you want to have someday!

☐ A beard

☐ Nose hair

☐ Ear hair

☐ Back hair

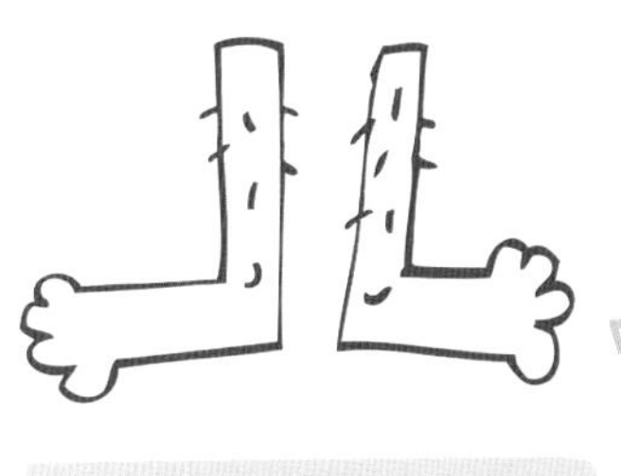

☐ Big shoes

☐ A gold tooth

DEAR DAD,

Here's a wristband for you!

Cut out each wristband to give to Dad!

I'm allowed to work on my computer
without being bothered

Draw a special wristband for your dad!

Cutout page

dear dad,

You're a real octopus!

Draw things your dad often holds in his hands. For example, a laptop, a garden hose, a book, a cellphone, a golf club, etc.

me
my dad loves ...
Color in all the items your dad loves.

Oh, and also:

dear dad, *On TV, you love watching:*

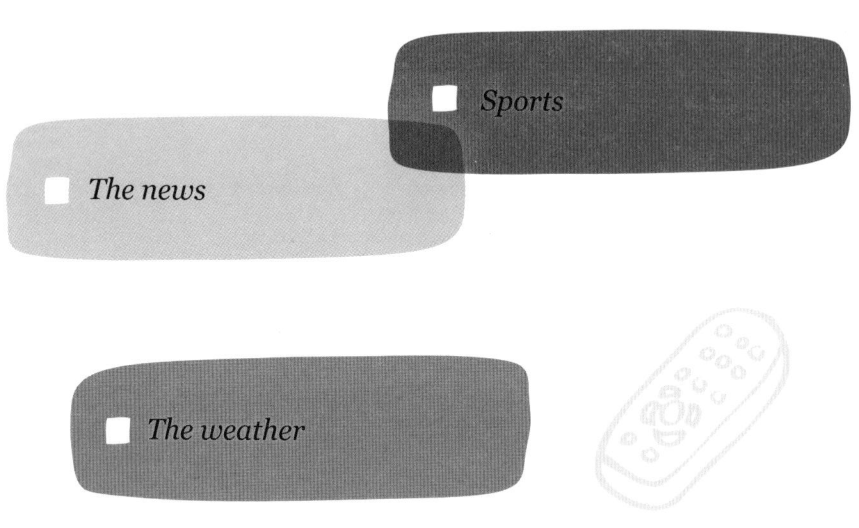

- [ ] *Sports*
- [ ] *The news*
- [ ] *The weather*

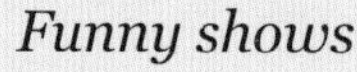

- [ ] *Funny shows*

- [ ] *Boring shows*
- [ ] *Things that happen in real life*
- [ ] *Whatever's on after I'm asleep*

Oh, and also:

(Write or draw what your dad loves to watch.)

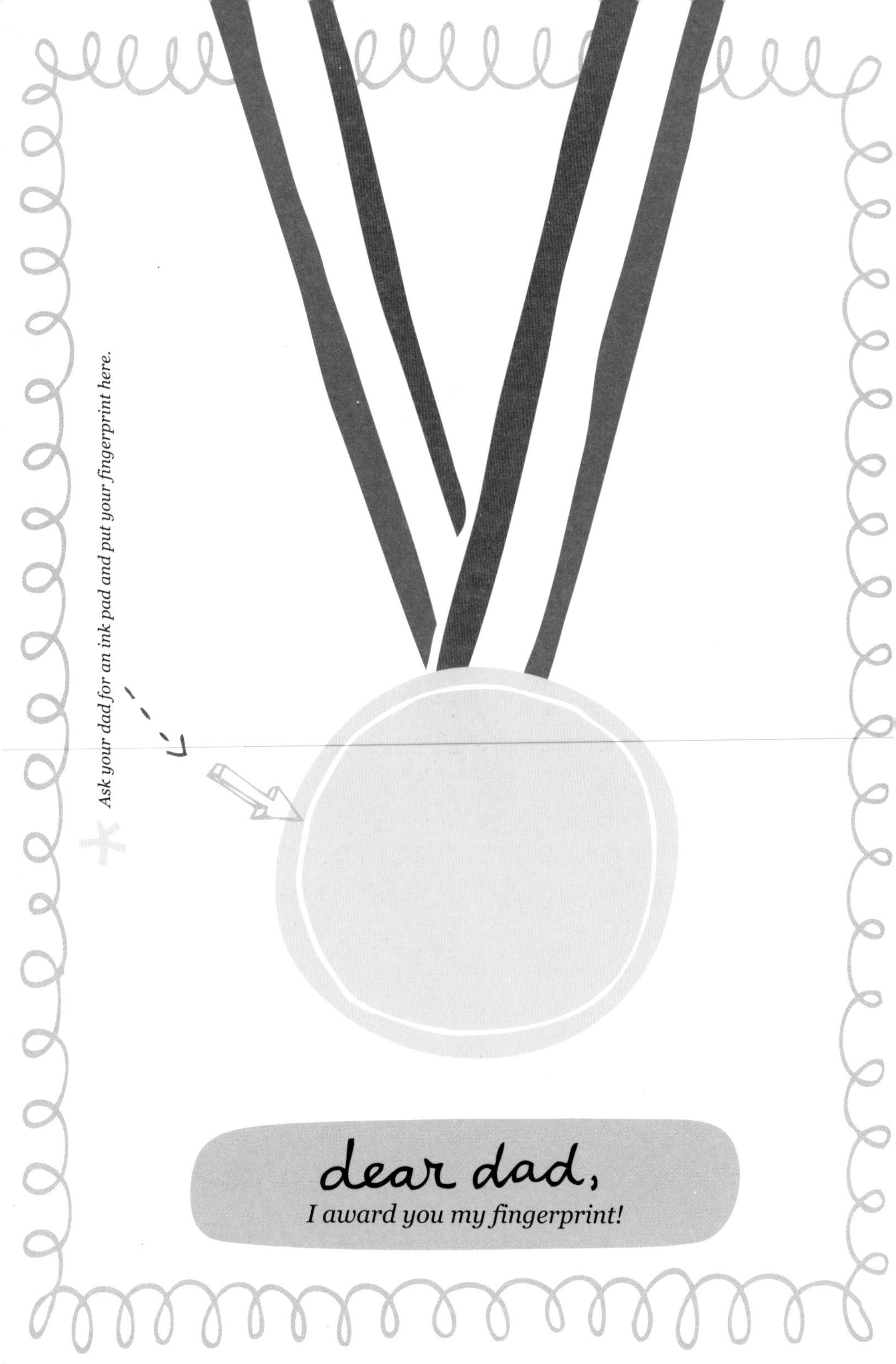
Ask your dad for an ink pad and put your fingerprint here.
dear dad,
I award you my fingerprint!